Rachel Carson
A LIFE OF RESPONSIBILITY

by Sheila Rivera

Lerner Publications Company • Minneapolis

Photo Acknowledgments

The images in this book are used with the permission of: PhotoDisc Royalty Free by Getty Images, p. 4; Ginger Wadsworth, p. 6; Yale Collection of American Literature, Beinecke Rare Book and Manuscript Library, pp. 7, 9, 13, 17, 18, 23; Used by the permission of Rachel Carson Council, Inc., p. 8; Rachel Carson Collection, College Archives, Chatham College, pp. 10, 14, 19; U.S. Fish and Wildlife Service, p. 12; Wendy W. Cortesi, p. 16; Agricultural Research Service, USDA, p. 20; © Galen Rowell/CORBIS, p. 22; © Getty Images, p. 24; © Alfred Eisenstaedt/Time Life Pictures/Getty Images, pp. 25, 27; AP/Wide World Photos, p. 26.
Cover: © Bettmann/CORBIS.

Lerner Publications Company
A division of Lerner Publishing Group
241 First Avenue North
Minneapolis, MN 55401 U.S.A.

Website address: www.lernerbooks.com

Words in **bold type** are explained in a glossary on page 31.

Library of Congress Cataloging-in-Publication Data

Rivera, Sheila, 1970-
    Rachel Carson : a life of responsibility / by Sheila Rivera.
      p. cm. — (Pull ahead books)
    Includes index.
    ISBN-13: 978-0-8225-6462-1 (lib. bdg. : alk. paper)
    ISBN-10: 0-8225-6462-9 (lib. bdg. : alk. paper)
    1. Carson, Rachel, 1907-1964–Juvenile literature. 2. Biologists–United
States–Biography–Juvenile literature. 3. Environmentalists–United
States–Biography–Juvenile literature. I. Title. II. Series.
QH31.C33R567 2007
570.92–dc22   2006025577

Manufactured in the United States of America
1 2 3 4 5 6 – JR – 12 11 10 09 08 07

Table of Contents

A Child in the Wilderness

Shhhhhhhh, listen. Do you hear that?
That rustling sound is the wind blowing
through the trees. That chirping noise is
a bird singing. These are the sounds
that Rachel Carson used to hear when
she was a child. When she grew up,
Rachel taught people to be **responsible**
and care for the environment.

Rachel Carson was born in 1907. Her family lived on a farm in Pennsylvania.

Rachel and her family lived in this farmhouse.

Rachel was the youngest child. When she was born, her brother and sister were already in school.

Rachel sits on her mother's lap next to her sister, Marian, and her brother, Robert.

Rachel and her dog rest in the yard.

Rachel spent a lot of time walking in the woods and fields near her house.

Rachel's mother loved nature. She taught Rachel to respect and love nature too.

Rachel and her mother read outside.

A Responsible Student

After high school, Rachel went to college. She was a responsible student. She studied day and night. Rachel graduated from college with **honors**.

Rachel received money to study more.
She studied sea animals.

Rachel and a friend look at a sponge.

Rachel studies sea life.

Rachel also worked at her college. She helped in the science **laboratory**.

Rachel and her parents when she was a child.

Responsible for Her Family

In 1935, Rachel's father died. Rachel was a responsible daughter. She began working a second job so she could take care of her mother.

Rachel wrote about sea animals like these jellyfish.

During the day, Rachel wrote **scripts** for a radio program about sea life.

At night, Rachel wrote nature articles for magazines and newspapers.

The next year, Rachel's sister, Marian, died. Marian had two young daughters.

Rachel's sister, Marian.

Rachel's family was important to her.

Rachel and her mother took care of the girls.

An airplane sprays chemicals on a field.

Caring for Nature

Rachel learned that people were hurting nature. They were using **pesticides** to kill insects that damaged **crops**. Rachel learned that these chemicals could hurt other animals and plants too.

Pesticides harmed this eggshell.

Rachel was responsible. She wrote a book about how pesticides hurt living things.

She said that people should be careful how they used pesticides.

Rachel wrote about the harm of using pesticides.

This woman sprays pesticide on an insect.

Some people did not want to stop using pesticides. They did not believe that pesticides were bad.

But Rachel continued to tell people about the harm they could do.

Rachel talked about nature to many people, including children.

Eventually the government made some pesticides **illegal**. People had to be more careful with the environment.

Rachel talks to lawmakers about the dangers of using pesticides.

Rachel studies a sea animal.

Rachel was responsible throughout her life. She taught people to respect and care for nature.

Rachel Carson Timeline

1907

Rachel Carson is born in Springdale, Pennsylvania.

1932

Rachel receives her master's degree in zoology from Johns Hopkins University.

1929

Rachel graduates from Pennsylvania College for Women.

1935
Rachel's father dies.

1962
Rachel writes her most famous book, *Silent Spring.*

1935
Rachel begins writing for the U.S. Bureau of Fisheries.

1936
Rachel's sister, Marian, dies. Her daughters come to live with Rachel.

1964
Rachel dies of cancer on April 14.

More about Rachel Carson

● Rachel Carson's book *The Sea Around Us* won the National Book Award. The book was also at the top of the *New York Times* Best Seller list for 39 weeks.

● After reading Rachel's book *Silent Spring*, President John F. Kennedy ordered an investigation of how chemicals might harm wildlife.

● The Fish and Wildlife Service named a refuge on the coast of Maine after Rachel. It is called the Rachel Carson National Wildlife Refuge.

Websites

RachelCarson.org
http://www.rachelcarson.org

The Rachel Carson Homestead
http://rachelcarsonhomestead.org

Rachel Carson National Wildlife Refuge
http://www.fws.gov/northeast/rachelcarson/carsonbio.html

A House for a Mouse

Written by Kathleen N. Daly
Illustrated by John P. Miller

A GOLDEN BOOK • NEW YORK
Western Publishing Company, Inc., Racine, Wisconsin 53404

Jonathan Mouse woke up with raindrops splashing on his head.

"It's time to find a real house to live in," he said. "Time to settle down!"

So into the street went Jonathan, whistling a cheerful tune and merrily jumping in and out of puddles.

Soon Jonathan was in the country.

The sun was shining, the flowers were blooming, a butterfly was flitting, and Duck was swimming in the pond with her new ducklings.

"Hello, Duck," said Jonathan. "Where do you live?"

"Here in the reeds," said Duck. "Come and see."

Duck and her ducklings paddled off. Jonathan Mouse jumped in after them.

"Oh, no!" said Jonathan. "This water is cold and wet!"

"Come and see my home," called Frog, diving under a lily pad.

"No, thanks," said Jonathan Mouse with a shiver. "Homes for ducks and frogs are TOO WET for a mouse!"

Jonathan Mouse was drying off in the sun when along came Bird.

"Come and see my home," said Bird.

Bird flew into a tree, and Jonathan scampered up after her.

"Oh, dear," said Jonathan. "It's a lovely nest for a bird—but birds can fly, and I can't! Thanks anyway!"

On his way down the tree
Jonathan saw Squirrel peering
out of his hole.

"Come on in," said Squirrel.

"No, thanks," said Jonathan.
"Homes for birds and squirrels are
much TOO HIGH UP for a mouse!"

Thump thump thump came the footsteps of a friendly brown bear.

"Come and see where I live," said Bear.

But when they got to Bear's cave, Jonathan Mouse felt a little scared.

"It's a lovely home for a bear," he said. "But it's much TOO BIG for a mouse. Thanks anyway!"

Hippity-hop, along came Rabbit.

"My house is much better," she said. "Come with me!"

When they got to Rabbit's hole, three baby rabbits squeaked and squealed and jumped all over Jonathan Mouse.

"Oh, dear," he said. "You are very nice rabbits in a very nice home—but you are much TOO NOISY for a mouse like me!"

As Jonathan Mouse sat panting outside the rabbit hole, who should come along but Fox.

Fox smiled a big, toothy smile at Jonathan.

"Come home with me," he said. "I'll show you a really nice home."

Jonathan Mouse followed Fox.

Soon they came to a hole, and Fox smiled some more.

"Do come in, dear Mouse," he said.

But Jonathan Mouse ran off, saying, "Thanks anyway, Fox—your TEETH are TOO BIG for me!"

Jonathan Mouse ran and ran until suddenly he bumped into another mouse and they both fell over.

"How nice to meet you, Jonathan Mouse," said the other mouse. "I hear you are looking for a house. So am I. My name is Emily Mouse. There's a farm here where everybody has a house. Let's go see!"

So off they went to visit the farm, Jonathan Mouse and Emily Mouse.

Yes, everyone on the farm had a home.
Dog lived in the doghouse.
Hen and Rooster and Chick lived in the chicken coop.

Horse lived in the stable.

Cow lived in the barn.

"But, there doesn't seem to be a house for a mouse," said Emily with a sigh.

"No," said Jonathan with another sigh.

From his perch up above, Blue Jay heard those sad little sighs.

"Come, follow me," he said. "I know the very place for you two."

"There!" said Blue Jay.

"Oh, what a pretty house!" said Emily. "It looks like a doll's house!"

"It just needs a little straightening up," said Jonathan.

Emily and Jonathan pushed and pulled and heaved
and grunted, and pretty soon that little house was as
straight up as any house ever was.

"Oh, thank you, Blue Jay," said Emily and Jonathan.

Jonathan found a toolbox, with tools just the right size for a mouse—or two.

Emily found some clothes, just the right size for a mouse—or two.

Then the two little mice swept and dusted and painted and tidied.

Jonathan sawed wood.
Emily planted a garden.

And when it grew dark, they put on their aprons
and cooked a fine stew—those two.

Then Emily Mouse and Jonathan Mouse sat down to supper in a house that was just exactly right for a mouse—or two.